PROGRESSIVE CHRISTIANITY

Caterpillar to Butterfly

From the cocoon of
GARY GOCEK

PERINTON, NEW YORK, USA

Published by Gary Gocek   https://gary.gocek.com/
Perinton, New York, United States of America.
ISBN: 979-8-9930106-0-1 paperback, 979-8-9930106-1-8 Kindle, 979-8-9930106-2-5 EPUB, 979-8-9930106-3-2 PDF
FIRST EDITION

*Do not be conformed to this world, but be
transformed by the renewing of your minds,
so that you may discern what is the good
and acceptable and perfect will of God.*
ROMANS 12:2

CONTENTS

ACKNOWLEDGEMENTS

The great mystery of the universe is how I got lucky enough to spend my life with Susan, Greg, Suki, Dan, Lauren, and all my family and friends. Thanks to my pastors and fellow Christians over the years—who should not be blamed—but at least I'm passionate! Thanks to my Education for Ministry seminar group members and the Rochester Writers and Books community writing group. Thanks be to God the Love, God the Word, and God the Holy Spirit.

Put on the whole armor of God, so that you may
be able to stand against the wiles of the devil.
EPHESIANS 6:11

PREFACE: THE CATERPILLAR

For a time, I thought I was a good Christian—
formerly a caterpillar wrapped in a cocoon of
half-belief, finally a disciple who had *figured it
out* and emerged as an evangelizing, loving
butterfly. Snowfalls appeared fluffier, summers
appeared greener, church appeared churchier,
and love appeared *agape*-ier. Alas, when my
emergent pride subsided, I noticed my journey
had not led to the kingdom of heaven on earth.
I noticed that many needs remained unmet, and
many people remained disinherited and un
loved. I thought I had emerged a butterfly of
Christianity wearing the full armor of God,
spreading the Good News to the still-cocooned,
but when my fog of pride lifted, the kingdom remained elusive.

In this book I reflect primarily on faith-driven
personal behaviors, and less on my role as a
member of a church. As a layperson praying to
discern my divinely assigned purpose, I must

coordinate my mission with my church's doctrine and leadership, but I am not at church every day. Churches set broad doctrinal directions, while I serve others and give thanks by using my unique gifts to do God's work.

You are welcome to make adjustments to support your own spiritual or secular perspectives, with the understanding that I accept two dogmas: the doctrine of the Holy Triadic Unity—the Holy Trinity—as the proper doctrine of God, and the doctrine of the two natures in one hypostasis—human and divine—of our Lord Jesus Christ. However, this is not a work of scholarly theology.

In 2025, I notice other Christians claiming their denominations are growing, even in the face of relentless media reports of widespread decline in church attendance, and a decline in the number of people claiming any religious affiliation at all. My own parish's attendance in 2025 has stagnated—we have not recovered to pre-pandemic levels and we're barely keeping pace with parishioner departures and passings. My parish welcomes families to our playground, walkers to our wooded property, and bargain-hunters to our rummage sales, but most do not return on Sunday mornings.

Among reportedly growing denominations, I observe mid-twentieth-century visions being preached to twenty-first-century Americans.

Adherents of these stale visions accept a hierarchical organization that excludes some demographic groups from leadership. Such an organization survives when the people at the top of the hierarchy are proud of their rankings, and when the people at the bottom are satisfied with the scraps beneath the masters' tables.

Businesses and armies require hierarchies, but Jesus discouraged human hierarchies among his followers. Exclusionary visions presumably create tensions within spiritual organizations when some members are offered more opportunities than others.

I consider whether I love my God, love my neighbor, live humbly, live righteously, and serve others in all I do. I reflect on the benefits and criticisms of a progressive approach—nondiscriminatory invitations to participation and leadership, and a radical humanization of everyone, including traditionally marginalized groups.

The kingdom is not established through inspirational platitudes. Inclusiveness and radical humanization are not the norm in America and require profound effort. In today's divisive political, social, and spiritual climate, prompt discernment and action are required.

Let's consider, then, a progressive approach so we may each work to emerge from our cocoons.

You shall love the Lord your God with
all your heart, and with all your soul,
and with all your mind.
MATTHEW 22:37

1) DO I LOVE MY GOD?

All I have are my gifts. They are divinely and uniquely given—different from *your* gifts. Some have been with me since birth, others were given to me at divinely appointed times. Compared to the infinite glory of the divine creator and gift-giver, my gifts and I are like grains of sand, not to be considered of more worth than you and yours. Paul wrote, *"For by the grace given to me I say to everyone among you not to think of yourself more highly than you ought to think, but to think with sober judgment, each according to the measure of faith that God has assigned"* (Romans 12:3). From my human perspective, though, my gifts are all I have, and I am called—by a higher power—to be thankful.

How can I, unworthy as I am in comparison to the divine giver, give thanks? The giver reveals the purpose for which my gifts were given through discernment on my part. Discernment is fraught with peril, since I am imperfect, but

James wrote, *"If any of you is lacking in wisdom, ask God…and it will be given you"* (James 1:5). James also instructs me to *"ask in faith"* (James 1:6)—that is, not for my own benefit but to fulfill a divine purpose. In summary, my gifts are divinely given and the giver helps me to discern my gifts and how to use them to fulfill the giver's purpose.

All Benefit Equivalently

There is no suggestion in the New Testament that any divine purpose will be for my personal benefit. This differs from Hebrew Scripture; the Old Testament frequently raises some humans above all others, such as Moses and David. Christians may quote the OT for certain purposes, but individuals in the NT who wonder about their purpose are reminded it is to serve the divine purpose. The Bible does not tell us Mary was created differently than other humans for the purpose of bearing Jesus. Mary was *"favored"* (Luke 1:28). Divine power overshadowed Mary and bestowed on her the gift of the conception of Jesus. Presumably, the birth was as painful as other births, *"…in pain you shall bring forth children"* (Genesis 3:16).

Jesus, incarnated as a human, wondered how he might avoid suffering, but then accepted the divine path, *"Abba, Father, for you all things are possible; remove this cup from me; yet, not what I want, but what you want"* (Mark 14:36).

In the OT, Isaac, son of Abraham, was rescued by an angel from being sacrificed (Genesis 22), but Jesus, son of the divine, accepted his own sacrifice to show the way to victory over death.

That's some heavy theology, so allow me to restate it. An individual claiming to have been divinely singled out to achieve only an earthly objective—one that does not describe a path to the divine kingdom of heaven on earth—clings to an Old Testament mentality. The claim may not be harmful behavior, but as a result, some people gain while others do not.

For example, if I prayerfully discern the divine gift of the ability to help old ladies across the street, and if I exercise that ability, then all of humanity will be a little closer to the kingdom. I didn't pick the gift, I didn't pick the task, my benefit is no greater than that of others, and—even as the old lady continues safely on her way—I remain a sinner who did good only through divine grace. The person claiming to have been divinely singled out for an earthly purpose did not prayerfully discern it.

Point / Counterpoint

Modern technology allows us to announce our accomplishments to the world, almost instantaneously. Social media, business, and politics are rife with individuals announcing great strides toward—something—but immediately, others counter the announcements by pointing out all the harm that will be done. The benefits and harms are defined by the individuals making their respective announcements. A familiar meme often follows, that Jesus didn't say whatever it was an announcement said. True enough, but such a meme doesn't explain anything. We know Jesus said, *"Sell your possessions, and give the money to the poor"* (Matthew 19:21). This is usually met with silence.

Too often after a big announcement, little is accomplished and the world plods along until the next big announcement. No one admits doing harm, no one admits the failure to achieve universal benefit, and no one admits any quid pro quo. Incumbents are reelected and not held accountable.

Of course, punishments are applied in egregious or criminal cases, but my main point is not against murders and the like. Also, of course, smart people achieve great things every day. However, even as inventions are invented, it's often unclear if the world becomes a better place. Improvements, if any, are usually not noticeable, and most grand announcements are forgotten. Sometimes, while helping one disinherited group, harm is transferred to other groups, with no accountability.

Why Don't We Do Better?

This chapter has been a wordy diatribe, but I think it is valid to recall the instruction of

James—to ask in faith for divine wisdom—rather than be satisfied with a couple of bucks and doing it again the next day. Recall also the meme attributed to Saint Augustine, *"Without God, we cannot. Without us, God will not."*

We rarely do better because it is so hard to love the divine. No matter what I do, it's never enough; there are always more needs to meet, and more oppressed to liberate. Neither the divine nor I are at fault, but I get overwhelmed. Only one person ever did enough, and he was crucified for it. I don't see myself going to *that* extreme.

You might be wondering if I think there is anything I have accomplished. Well, I didn't write 9,000 words without at least a little prayerful discernment. I wrote a book!

You shall love your neighbor as yourself.
MATTHEW 22:39

2) DO I LOVE MY NEIGHBOR?

My neighbors are themselves divine gifts, for whom I must be thankful. We are social animals, which can result in tensions, but we cannot live separately from each other. Jesus said, *"For where two or three are gathered in my name, I am there among them"* (Matthew 18:20). Jesus was addressing disagreements between small numbers of people and their need to work together to toward resolution. We are not alone, and Jesus helps to maintain good relationships, and these relationships are to be cherished.

I cannot restrict my love—*agape*—to neighbors who happen to look or think like me. I am a progressive evangelist, but it is not acceptable for me to dislike those whose doctrinal beliefs differ from mine. We might disagree with each other, but we shouldn't dislike each other.

As some have ignored this, we have too few young people serving in government at the highest levels because the entrenched elders refuse to relinquish their privileges, and treat young politicians with disdain. One-percenters pledge huge sums to reelection campaigns, maintaining the status quo.

Why do patriarchal systems in business, government, and organized religion survive? These days, few Americans consider it necessary for a bride to be "given away", so why do we still do a double-take at a wedding where the bride is not given away?

Ancient Scripture is pervasively patriarchal; therefore, love for a neighbor in 2025 requires interpreting Scripture from a modern cultural perspective. After all, it was never OK for David to take Bathsheba for himself by sending Uriah into battle (2 Samuel 11), and Jesus's choice of male apostles continues to be misinterpreted to discriminate against women when selecting today's Christian leaders.

The Abuse of Women

The worst problem in America and the world is the constant and systemic abuse of women, along with trafficking and the abuse of children. No matter how bad your day was, there is no worse example of acting without love than to beat a woman because dinner is late.

The abuse is emotional, physical, and sexual. Popular fiction glamorizes this abuse, magnified with the help of AI and modern video techniques. Abusers—mostly men—use their divine gifts of creativity to imagine increasingly malevolent ways to harm the vulnerable.

Wars and disasters exacerbate abuse when victims and their dependents struggle to meet basic human needs. The most vulnerable suffer the most. However, abuse occurs every day, even in outwardly quiet and comfortable, first-world communities.

Sources of statistics are easily found. A third of women worldwide are sexually abused, and other issues. Researchers work to cure cancer, and nonprofits work to reduce hunger, but abuse is the elephant in the room, hidden and ignored when it should be exposed and addressed. There are shelters and legal options, but those can be extraordinary steps for vulnerable individuals.

Sex

In the epistles attributed to Paul where passages address fornication and the like, contemporary readers often conclude these pertain to homosexuality. In 2025, nonconsensual and rough behavior must also be considered.

The #MeToo movement has led to positive changes. Women are becoming willing to call out unacceptable behavior. Men are becoming aware of how the lines separating acceptable and unacceptable behavior have moved.

During an episode of NPR's *Fresh Air*—see the link in my bibliography—Veralyn Williams

said, "You respect somebody's consent because you respect their humanity." Her point
was that consent is not just a legal construct.
Partners often think asking for consent *checks
a box*, implying a purely physical approach to
sex, without empathy for the other's feelings.

Also, during the episode, Gen-Z writer Tobias Hess used the term "porny" to refer to sexual practices learned from watching porn.
Hess's female friends had complained of being
choked by men in the course of a first sexual
encounter; the women had consented to sex,
but were uncomfortable with the unexpected
roughness. Hess gave no statistics, but anec-
dotally, young men are learning bedroom behavior from explicit video games.

To be fair, most people, most of the time,
do not experience nonconsensual porn sex on
a first date. Just the same, we have access to
countless hours of unrestricted, high-def entertainment, and for many, this has resulted in a
tolerance for transactional, dehumanizing behavior. The consumption of this entertainment,
extramarital sex, or prostitution, does not necessarily lead to damnation, but the commandment to love—humanize—my neighbor is not
set aside just because I am feeling frisky.

Incels and Femcels

In 2025, anecdotal observations suggest that
young men are exhibiting effeminacy induced

by ADHD medications. Women find this unattractive, but then accuse the remaining men of ungentlemanly behavior or exaggerated masculinity. We hear of *incels*—involuntarily celibate men who blame women for their lack of romantic success. Recently, we hear of *femcels*—female celibates—self-deprecating and exasperated by the whole situation. Simultaneously, oversexualized media are glorified by these supposedly celibate masses. The legalization of cannabis products continues to spread, as if society's gridlock might be resolved simply by placing us all under the influence.

I'm not referring to the extremes of war and neo-Nazis. I am referring to our every-day coworkers and classmates. We just don't seem to like each other very much.

LGBTQ

In 2025, fewer than ten percent of Americans identify as LGBTQ. I identify as a cisgender straight man. Definitions and identities are fluid. The New Testament authors didn't consider "gender identity" and I discern no divine opinion from the Bible. I am frustrated with the attitudes of LGBTQ and non-LGBTQ individuals alike.

My encounters with LGBTQ individuals have been positive, and they are as welcome on my Christian journey as anyone else. Anyone who denigrates or marginalizes LGBTQ individuals because of their identities is not on my progressive path; I'll address that shortly. However, I am also frustrated with LGBTQ individuals who are not on a progressive journey.

Mainly, I refer to LGBTQ individuals who exhibit an overwhelming focus on the self—a self-centered, defensive approach with cathartic essays about the pain of ostracization, protest marches and rainbow flags, and trans women competing in athletic contests against biological women. On the whole, their families and society aren't improved by these defensive behaviors.

The defensive approach sidesteps the "second greatest commandment", to love the neighbor. Neighbors don't always seem to love each other—I'm getting to that—but it doesn't help anyone to hate them back.

At the same time, I fear for the well-being of my trans friends who aren't able to identify their genders, possibly for years. The suicide rate of individuals in that predicament is a shocking 40 percent. While cisgender straight individuals question why there are so many interracial couples on TV, trans individuals wonder why there are couples at all. They don't know which restroom to use.

In the first century, Paul and the people to whom he evangelized did not use phrases like "sexual orientation" and "gender identity". Biblical references to sexuality are not comparable to a discussion of these modern scientific and sociological concepts. Paul observed bad behavior—morally troubling even by progressive standards—but he did not provide us with cell phone videos and we don't know the full context. Paul's understanding, even if divinely inspired, was different from ours. I lean toward the interpretation—see Powell in my bibliography—that Paul's prohibitions do "not necessarily apply to responsible partnerships between persons who are homosexual in terms of a basic (possibly genetic) orientation."

Consider also that there are 7,957 canonical verses in the New Testament, give or take a few depending on denominational adjustments. My progressive interpretation is that two verses in Romans do not deserve more influence than the other 99 percent of all verses, given Paul's different understanding.

Rape, sexual abuse, trafficking, female genital mutilation, child abuse, and other nonconsensual victimizations are damnable today, but Paul's adjectives—*unnatural* and *shameful*—likely described a divergence from righteousness rather than a perceived catastrophe brought about by physical acts during a drunken orgy. In Paul's society, martial law prevailed and a quarter of the people were slaves.

In the face of all that, he dedicated himself to evangelizing a path to eternal salvation. I am not convinced Paul hoped his most memorable lesson would be to eternally condemn gays.

In summary, I am frustrated when cis-gender straight individuals use ancient Scripture to marginalize loving and productive individuals and couples today. Respectful bedroom activity is not a problem. According to Matthew, Jesus said we are to love, including even LGBTQ individuals. LGBTQ individuals, for their part, need to heed Matthew's Gospel as well, and to steer their self-centered defensiveness toward a love for others. Paul's words were not intended as an eternal diatribe against LGBTQ individuals, and interpreting them as such perverts the behavior of both traditionalists and LGBTQ individuals.

Do nothing from selfish ambition or
conceit, but in humility regard others
as better than yourselves.
PHILIPPIANS 2:3

3) DO I LIVE HUMBLY?

If I presume to possess divine gifts, I betray the verse above concerning humility. I atone for this betrayal by prayerfully discerning a divine purpose and fulfilling it through the use of my gifts.

If I place my neighbor below me in any way, then I am not loving my neighbor. If I interpret Scripture to support the ranking of people, then I am not loving my neighbor. Jesus encouraged his followers to choose less honored places at a table to avoid the embarrassment of being asked to move when VIPs arrived.

Some readers believe the Twelve Apostles were male because Jesus recognized boundaries preventing women from this role, but consider that two individuals state the *Christological confession*—that Jesus is the divine Messiah: Peter in Mark 8:29 and Martha in John 11:27. Eleven of the Apostles never used the word "messiah" in this way, but Martha, a female, discerned this truth. See Bass in my bibliography.

Jesus, John the Baptist, and Paul were each circumcised at the age of eight days, in accordance with Genesis 17:12. Why, then, did they establish baptism by water as the ritual of initiation for Christianity? In my opinion, baptism was chosen for Christianity because it includes females. Circumcision is patriarchal, exclusionary, and raises men above women. It is not antisemitic for me to make this claim because circumcision is not intrinsic to Semitic heritage. Circumcision is patriarchal and a hard tradition to shake after three thousand years. See my bibliography under *Research, in a manner of speaking*.

When women are excluded and marginalized, it is either due to intentional male selfishness or subconscious lack of respect. In both cases, men who marginalize women feel superior, feel entitled to the benefits, and will justify the means to these ends. This marginalization lacks humility.

1 Timothy vs. Galatians

Church leadership should not be limited to a gender or sexual orientation. See Funmi Akinwale in my bibliography. At issue is, *"I permit no woman to teach or to have authority over a man; she is to keep silent"* (1 Timothy 2:12).

This is a translation of an ancient Greek

epistle widely believed to be pseudepigra-phal—written in Paul's name by someone else—a common literary practice in the first century in honor of a teacher. The author pro-vided little context: we don't know if a false teacher was influencing local Christians, or if the author was referring to specific women, or if the author intended to refer to all women for all time, or if there was some other patriarchal in-tent. Scholars debate its relevance to modern social relationships and church leadership.

I give greater weight to the notable verse in Galatians, as does Nicholas Gold—see my bib-liography. *"There is no longer Jew or Greek, there is no longer slave or free, there is no longer male and female; for all of you are one in Christ Jesus"* (Galatians 3:28). This epistle, in contrast to 1 Timothy, is considered to be au-thentically Pauline.

1 Timothy described household relation-ships between wives and husbands, and Gala-tians described spiritual relationships between humans and the divine. The two addressed dif-ferent contexts and were probably written by different authors. However, I don't think those inspired writers wanted us to believe we'll all be rewarded equally in heaven as long as women are marginalized on earth. Churches have hier-archies and we should respect our assigned church leaders, but assignments should not be

based on arbitrary discrimination.

In Galatians, Paul responded to centuries of patriarchy. A Socratic saying and a Talmudic men's prayer express gratefulness for having been born male rather than female—see Palvanov in my bibliography. The inspired writers of the New Testament gave us the virtue of humility with the verse from Philippians above, and rebutted Socrates and the Talmud with the egalitarianism in Galatians.

We should not interpret 1 Timothy as a divinely inspired and eternally mean-spirited snipe at women.

Darwinian Vision

The secular media report declines in mainline church attendance, but a few denominations claim significant growth. In particular, some report measurable growth in attendance among young men.

I prompted an AI bot for more information and it referred me to psychologist and author Jordan Peterson. Peterson wrote, "Dominance hierarchies have been an essentially permanent fixture of the environment to which all complex life has adapted." Peterson's objective is to persuade young men that:

• Assertive masculinity will get the jobs, the money, and the women.

• This is the optimal and anthropologically validated way to structure a society.

The AI bot made the connection between Peterson and churches because some young men are attracted to denominations providing a corresponding hierarchical environment. These men, having achieved secular success, are looking for cooperative young women.

In Peterson's environment, men compete with each other to establish their places in a hierarchy; the higher up a man rises, the greater his variety of choices—of jobs, social circles, and women. Women compete with each other to be chosen by successful men. The most attractive women—however a community defines attractiveness—are selected the most quickly and by the men highest in the hierarchy.

Peterson's world of cavemen competing for mates is not for the mindless or fainthearted. Men who aren't competitive or who choose less impressive careers rank lower and choose later from the pool of women. Women who focus on personal achievements rather than beauty attract fewer male suitors.

This *patriarchal Darwinism* is encouraged by some denominations and justified through medieval Scriptural interpretations. This approach has undeniably achieved some success, but it is not humble—nor are its clerical adherents.

As God's chosen ones, holy and beloved,
clothe yourselves with compassion, kind-
ness, humility, meekness, and patience.
COLOSSIANS 3:12

4) DO I LIVE RIGHTEOUSLY?

Living righteously is not merely about avoiding bad behavior. It is also important to do good. I am a sinner and cannot do good except by divine grace, so I must prayerfully seek to discern what is good. There is a systematic way to do this, by practicing a set of disciplines. I will discuss four—worship, prayer, study, vocation—but the list is flexible, provided there is a thoughtful framework. For example, if I have prayerfully identified music as important to me, that can become a discipline, one for which I set aside time to maintain my relationship with the divine. The following disciplines are widely affirmed as a foundational group:

Worship

Even though Sabbath-day church attendance in America has declined over the last few decades, it is a place where a young worker looking for a mentor can sit next to a CEO. This is a valuable opportunity missed by the un-churched.

Christianity is, at its core, a social en-deavor. Some spiritual practices can be done in solitude, but regular worship with others—to-gether offering thanks for their divine gifts—is uplifting and refreshing. The Abrahamic reli-gions follow this model. Alternatives that sup-port solo worship—or none at all—tend to be spiritually stunted.

Prayer

College degrees and trade certifications lead to success, and young adults work hard. I am no longer a young worker, and it was not my intent to denigrate them in my comments above.

These days, however, entertaining distrac-tions are always at hand. Text a friend a photo of dinner, or stream the latest episode of the re-ality show *du jour*, or bet on the outcome of the next three-pointer—there's hardly time to pray, meditate, or reflect—whatever one might call it. This discipline is often practiced in solitude, but it parallels group worship. Continue to nurture a relationship with the divine, even when alone.

Study

On the whole, Americans in 2025 read less for personal enjoyment—outside of work and school—than a few decades ago, and your time with this book is appreciated. Reliance on AI for creative work is growing, including emails, drawings, and summaries. Most American workers have no idea how AI actually works, but they use the free time provided by AI to catch up on that reality show—assuming the AI doesn't report back to the boss. Not all students and workers are cheating, but the efficiencies of AI are alluring.

If there is less critical thinking occurring in general, it presumably extends to church-seeking or avoidance. There are countless variations of Christianity to be compared and contrasted. Churches that make promises that seem too good to be true, or preach exceptionalism for particular demographics, should be viewed with suspicion.

Spiritual understanding rarely develops in isolation. I didn't grasp the depth of Christianity until I read the Bible from Genesis to Revelation, accompanied by historical commentary, diverse perspectives, fellow seekers, and the guidance of mentors. This applies to students of Abrahamic traditions, neo-pagans, and committed humanists.

Vocation

People who volunteer, travel, or participate in the arts meet others with a variety of gifts and opinions. People who spend their time or their devices tend to engage with like-minded individuals. This isn't inherently wrong—they are still interacting—but the exchanges tend to be self-reinforcing.

Contemporary Christian Music is a form of self-centeredness. CCM lyrics don't explain their frequent use of hallelujahs, or why Jesus is a king—CCM is for people who are already Christian. Our practices should instead reach out to consider love, humility and service, beyond repeating the buzzwords. Certainly, some CCM fans reach out, but CCM can seem more about the music than the message.

We who worship corporately do not conclude our services thinking we're done for the week. We are reminded that our worship space, while special and refreshing, is part of the overall divine creation. Inside and outside the space, we are called to fulfill our divine purpose through the use of our divinely given gifts, as discerned through prayer.

Whether through these four disciplines—or a prayerfully discerned, personalized set—these practices express gratitude for divine gifts. This gratitude is central to righteousness. Perhaps it's self-serving to call writing a book a form of study—but if these disciplines fade from public consciousness, so too does our awareness of others' needs.

*Let each of you look not to your own inter-
ests, but to the interests of others.*
PHILIPPIANS 2:4

5) DO I SERVE OTHERS IN ALL I DO?

It's not about me—it's about everyone else.

Paul's verse above reminded the Philippians—and us—that service was very important
to Christian converts in the first century.

The USA was founded by self-reliant pio-
neers, and the Constitution protects individuals
from the government chosen by a majority.
However, while caring for themselves in com-
petition against the majority, individualists
rarely limit themselves to essentials so they can
dedicate the rest to the good of the community.
That's what Paul asks—I cannot ignore my individual well-being, but constitutional protec-
tions are not intended to be exclusionary. I
should not reject everyone else.

Progressive Christianity is the theological
antithesis of constitutional individualism. Christianity's human-divine incarnation—Jesus—
was sacrificed for the cause. This can be scary,
emerging from my safe cocoon—Jesus showed
how hard Christianity is, and I am asked to take

up my own cross. I cannot fully meet the standard set by Jesus, but I have to pray and try.

Psycho-commentator Jordan Peterson's dominance hierarchy theory—mentioned earlier—promises rewards, but they are earthly. Peterson theorizes it's the natural order of the universe. It's true the relationship between humans and the divine is inherently hierarchical, but the New Testament authors recognized only two levels—divine and human. When Revelation says God *"will wipe every tear from their eyes,"* that refers to everyone, not just to the fittest. The only way to achieve that is for everyone to chip in. Evolution promises survival until mortality catches up; Jesus promises eternal salvation. For me, dominance hierarchies lack empathy for those who don't submit to my dominance. That doesn't seem like a way to express thanks for my divine gifts.

I dwell on Jordan Peterson because his theories are consistent with the doctrines of traditionalist denominations experiencing growth. His work has received widespread negative criticism.

Modern Protest is not Service.

In America in 2025, mass protests have enjoyed a revival, and are outwardly concerned with the wellbeing of the larger community. Large-scale protests are legal and a historically honored tradition, especially when organizers promote nonviolent community activism. They talk the talk, but I doubt how much anyone is truly served. The protest signs are funny and the hats are silly, but they don't persuade elected officials or CEOs to change. The largest protests in big cities are overshadowed in the media by hired agitators and vandals.

Small-scale protests are ineffective because they focus on one concern to the point of illegality, such as blocking access to healthcare clinics. Small protests get publicity, but often kick the can down the road, and sometimes hurt other marginalized people.

Any protest typically involves two vehemently opposed sides. For example, when an antiwar protester claims oppression, another protester claims self-defense; eventually, protesters give up in the face of propaganda and the intractability of it all, and redirect their attention to local or tangible concerns—like potholes on Main Street. The goal should be to wipe tears from the eyes of everyone, not just from the eyes of those named on a picket sign.

> But false prophets also arose among
> the people, just as there will be false
> teachers among you.
> 2 PETER 2:1

DIFFICULTIES AND CRITICISMS

How many progressives does it take to change a light bulb? *One, but the need to change the bulb must be prayerfully discerned alongside cultural, scientific, linguistic, historical, and sociological frameworks.*

Christian leaders in the first century struggled to establish doctrinal and behavioral norms, and since then, to establish consistent interpretations. Over the last century, traditionalists have criticized progressive Christianity for a variety of reasons.

There is no universally accepted definition of progressive Christianity. Progressive movements have adopted various labels: alt worship, emerging or emergent, modernist or post-modernist, missional, and the Social Gospel movement. My position aligns with liberal Protestantism, emphasizing critical dogma as I have stated. This is not the same as megachurch approaches providing modern music, prosperity theology, and traditional family values.

Mainstream news articles—such as by Peter Smith in my bibliography—have reported declines in attendance among denominations incorporating non-traditional elements such as female leadership and LGBTQ inclusion, while being accused of insufficient doctrinal rigidity. Journalists attempt to remain neutral, but when they avoid passing judgement, readers assume the journalists mean that progressive doctrines cause the drops in attendance.

However, attendance isn't the only objective of any spirituality—marginalization and exclusion should be called out as unloving. Progressive theological interpretations are sometimes criticized, but there is no universal, scholarly agreement.

While some denominations have had some success growing some demographics, the successes are offset by weaknesses in other areas. The media do not typically ask the general population which doctrinal mix would fill the pews. It is questionable to assume that the general population yearns for patriarchal, exclusionary doctrines.

Machen

The seminal criticism of evolving Christianity was written by J. Gresham Machen in 1923—see my bibliography. For Machen and me, the biblical canon is immutable, but I argue that exegesis evolves. In 1923, Machen expressed concern that, over time, progressive Christianity's interpretations and lifestyles would be ever-evolving due to advances in science, sociology, historical discoveries, and linguistics— bad, according to Machen. I disagree—cultural changes require constant reflection on Christian doctrine.

Machen was concerned that modernists deny penal substitutionary atonement (PSA)— that Jesus died for humanity. I don't deny PSA, but it presents us with a dilemma: the wrathful God the Father forgives us only after we repent, while the loving Jesus the Son forgives us freely. *Wrathful* and *loving* are different, but the Father and Son are dogmatically of one substance in the Holy Trinity. To resolve this dilemma in 2025, I focus on Christ's victory over death, which promises eternal salvation for all.

Repentance is still important; I am a sinner and I will be judged. However, divine love doesn't begin only after I repent; it has always been waiting for me to stop denying it. See Matthew J. Distefano in my bibliography.

This is as deep into the weeds as a Christian can get, so consult with your pastor for guidance. I'm a progressive trying to address Machen's historically significant criticism. If I adhere to the two dogmas—of God as a trinity and Jesus as both human and divine—and if I justify my lifestyle through the study of Scripture, then Machen and I would have a common starting point. I benefit from a century's worth of theological reflection since 1923.

Media Commentary

There has been a loss of trust in the media and politicians across demographics. Clergy abuse scandals have bred widespread cynicism and bankrupted dioceses. These are problems for progressives and traditionalists.

Paraphrasing William A. Galston of the Wall Street Journal, cultural change creates demands to which religion and theology are pushed to respond. Churches can barely influence behavior among their members, and have even less influence over, say, the community divorce rate, or violence against women, or the approval rate of business loans for Black applicants, or the manipulation of banking rules to conduct warrantless investigations of political foes. The progressive approach is to recognize injustices and promote the discipline needed to avoid them.

Media articles and theological critiques tend to focus on systemic, denominational doctrine. I suggest that individuals are equipped to evaluate and improve our own respective behaviors—even as we coordinate our journeys with our churches. An individual in a position to put governmental pressure on bankers knows when a policy is unfair or vindictive. An individual inclined to beat a spouse knows it is wrong and unloving. I need to internalize doctrine to be able to personally discern right from wrong.

Pushback Against Progressivism in 2025

Jesus had little to say about *churches*. He taught *individuals* to love God and neighbor.

I focus on individual behavior, but churches and denominations are systems in which individuals operate as members. Regarding the decline in church attendance in America, especially among progressive denominations, might members believe there is something flawed in progressive systems?

Racism and sexism persist in 2025, defying years of progressive efforts, legislatively and socially. *Woke* progressives have rushed to accuse others of unethical behavior. In response, traditionalist detractors have rushed to claim reverse discrimination, that critical race theory labels patriotic Americans as incorrigible racists, and that progressives want to defund the police.

Traditionalist authors Allie Beth Stuckey and Joe Rigney address important issues, but resort to light-bulb jokes. *How many progressives does it take to rescue a drowning person? None, progressives jump in and drown in empathetic solidarity.* Stuckey and Rigney can sell this fluff only to other traditionalists. Here are my thoughts on their issues:

• The claim that any slave or slave owner ever benefited from slavery epitomizes callous dehumanization. Famine is inexcusable.

• Women are too often marginalized and abused, but men should not be presumed to be evil just because they are men.

• Abortion should be the last choice. The proper approach is to provide choice, justice, and comfort to all stakeholders: fetus, mother, father, society, and healthcare providers.

• You may refer to me by any pronoun; it won't change my identity. I must respect others, and avoid self-defensive behaviors that make productive relationships impossible.

• Trans women have not clearly demon-strated injustice as they enter athletic competi-tions against biological women. Any competitor might feel outclassed at times, but the manipu-lative exploitation of loopholes can seem unfair.

• As I stated earlier, respectful bedroom activity is not a problem. We don't know the full contexts in which Paul wrote about sex.

• The *Good Samaritan* (Luke 10) helped the injured person even though the two didn't live within the same borders. Jesus and Paul may have accommodated border regulation, but we should avoid causing harm and instead use our gifts to help meet their needs of others.

Tax Exemptions

Most American churches and other religious organizations are exempt from most federal and regional taxes. The Internal Revenue Service imposes some restrictions and reporting requirements, though the ban on political endorsements from the pulpit was lifted in 2025.

Regarding government taxation, Powell, as cited in my bibliography, notes the following:

• Jesus focused on loving God.

• Apocalyptic texts such as Revelation encouraged opposition, though this was historically directed at Nero.

• Paul encouraged cooperation with government officials for the good of the community.

Taxation and representation are closely linked. While tax exemptions help maintain the separation of church and state, they diminish the influence of churches and pastors in governmental affairs.

These exemptions influence progressives and traditionalists alike. Christians often believe they are called to speak truth to power. Just as thankfulness should accompany prayer, support for the community should accompany political speech and activism.

Radical is Difficult

Progressive Christianity focuses on humility and service, and rejects marginalization and human hierarchies, but practicing it is difficult. It's practically un-American to reject self-centered individualism. Progressives who make radical sacrifices can find themselves in the minority, swimming against a current of entrenched traditionalism.

"Do you think that I have come to bring peace to the earth? No, I tell you, but rather division!" (Luke 12:51-52) Jesus was pointing to the reality that there are ways to show love and gratitude—and ways to reject them. Such rejection must be defied—and defied now—thus the division. Poet Mary Oliver asked, "Can one be passionate about the just, the ideal, the sublime, and the holy, and yet commit to no labor in its cause?"

It is hard to speak truth at all, and even harder to speak truth to power, or to friends and relatives. The items in the next chapter may seem overwhelming when taken together, but they can be approached one at a time.

*So if anyone is in Christ, there is a new
creation: everything old has passed
away; see, everything has become new!*
2 CORINTHIANS 5:17

EPILOGUE: THE BUTTERFLY

Trust, Privacy, Security

To emerge from our safe cocoons, we must
trust that Scripture—interpreted over centuries
through labor, sacrifice, theological reflection,
and divine inspiration—establishes guidelines
for behavior that lead to a more just and com-
passionate world. My support for inclusiveness
and radical humanization can be criticized, but
I won't be convinced Jesus ever taught that
women are unfit to lead a church or that it's acceptable—as discussed earlier—for men to
choke women on a first date.

Every day, I protect my personal privacy
and security—bank accounts, mobile devices,
and home security. This is a fact of modern life.
Love, though, is risky. To love and be loved is
to be seen and touched—physically, spiritually,
vulnerably. This is the cost of walking the path
toward the kingdom of heaven on earth.

Evangelize

I have researched how some denominations are experiencing growth among young male members. Here, I reflect on how to nourish legitimate individual needs while performing neighbor-loving community service. Whatever you believe, evangelize it!

Inclusion and Leadership

Dominance hierarchies marginalize the lower ranks—usually women, LGBTQ individuals, and non-dominant racial groups. Christian dioceses and parishes need to promote inclusion and justice.

Businesses need hierarchy. Someone must be responsible for maintaining a stable business model to keep employees productive.

However, in our churches and homes, the New Testament teaches us to watch over a wider range of needs, from physical safety to hunger to spirituality, and everything in between. Church wasn't built as a place for men to compete for leadership as a means of controlling access to women.

Progressive and traditionalist churches may share similar demographics, but it is the progressive ethic of self-sacrificing love for God and neighbor that makes the difference. When competitiveness is sacrificed for inclusion, fellow progressives become co-laborers in watching over one another's needs. The relationship with the divine—with its spiritual promise—takes time to develop, but redeems what might feel like a sacrifice of individual gain.

Relationships in Moderation

As with parish governance, a relationship between two people—especially when it deepens beyond the platonic—should be grounded in inclusiveness and radical humanization. Don't expect sex too soon. Don't expect marriage too soon. Begin with gentleness.

The Golden Rule

"In everything do to others as you would have them do to you" (Matthew 7:12). The familiarity of this verse must not be allowed to distract us from its depth. We are all sinners. We are called to repent and to recognize the repentance of others.

Consider, for example, pedophiles and neo-Nazis, among the most extreme transgressors. They will be judged, but when they repent, we must recognize that a diseased hatefulness had overcome them. They are broken—and they need healing. Protect the victims, but the perpetrators need us to provide radical humanization. This is the depth of the challenge.

Go to Church, Keep the Sabbath

For Christians, a worship service provides parishioners with an opportunity to compare the ways in which we express thanks for our divine gifts and the ways we work to fulfill our divine purposes. Apart from worship, we can attend volunteer meetings, book clubs, and other gatherings to maintain relationships with people who are doing good things.

Kids

One way to learn selfless service to others is by raising children. Infants, in particular, are completely dependent on parental love. Constant dedication as a parent—through childhood and beyond—is a profound service to the community.

Progressiveness other than Christian

Non-Christians, including atheists, can be inclusive humanists. However, I can be trusted to justify my beliefs through an understanding of biblical Scripture. A Christian reader might disagree with the details of my personal theology, but we would both be awaiting eternal salvation on the last day.

An atheist can shift from progressiveness to conservatism to dominance hierarchies at will; critics can disagree, but no higher power or authoritative foundation had been suggested.

Anyone who can be trusted to promote peace and justice, and to extend the definition of *consensual* to include empathy, is on a similar path to mine.

Volunteer

Find a way to help others without expecting a reward. Serve food at a homeless shelter. Volunteer as an usher or docent for a local arts organization. Do pro bono legal work. Join the volunteer fire department. Protest if you think it helps—but then volunteer to assist refugees.

We can't all quit our jobs and walk from town to town like Paul, evangelizing the Good News. The first-century lifestyle has largely become a metaphor. However, video games, football, and visits to the cannabis dispensary do not lead to any kingdoms.

Emerge

Thanks for bearing with this blend of frustration and hope. Most of us think good thoughts most of the time, but never quite emerge as the righteous Christian butterflies we aspire to be. In all humility, I'm still trying—and succeed only by divine grace. Christianity is a journey; some of us may emerge one day, only to face setbacks the next and return to the cocoon. You may have heard this as *dying to self and rising anew in Christ*. Sounds progressive to me.

*As he peered ahead into the great land that
stretched before him, the way seemed long.
But the sky was bright, and he somehow
felt he was headed in the right direction.*
STUART LITTLE, E. B. WHITE, 1945

BIBLIOGRAPHY—ANNOTATED

Books and Prose

Green, Joel B. (general editor). *The CEB Study
Bible with Apocrypha.* Nashville: Common English Bible, 2013.
   This is an American English translation.

Machen, J. Gresham. *Christianity and Liberalism: A Classic Defense of Biblical Faith Against
Modernist Theology.* New York: The MacMillan
Company, 1923.
   Machen's credentials are impeccable. This is
   the seminal criticism of what Machen referred
   to as the "modern church.", though dated.

Oliver, Mary. *What I Have Learned So Far,* from
New and Selected Poems Volume 2. Boston:
Beacon Press, 2005.

Oxford University Press. *The New Oxford Annotated Bible, New Revised Standard Version*

with the Apocrypha, an Ecumenical Study Bible, Fully Revised Fourth Edition. New York: Oxford University Press, 2010.
  NRSV is the primary American English translation used by the Episcopal Church USA.

Peterson, Jordan. *12 Rules for Life: An Antidote to Chaos.* Toronto: Random House Canada, 2018.
  Survival of the fittest—it works for lobsters.

Powell, Mark Allan. *Introducing the New Testament, A Historical, Literary, and Theological Survey, Second Edition.* Grand Rapids: Baker Academic, 2018.
  A general analysis of the New Testament.

Powell, Mark Allan. *Supplement to Introducing the New Testament, Second Edition.* Grand Rapids: Baker Academic, 2018.
  Over 2000 pages of supplemental articles.
  "Church and State: The Ethic of Resistance," "The Ethic of Subordination," "The Ethic of Critical Distancing": These articles explain New Testament approaches to the relationship between church and state. Should I pay taxes? Depends on who I ask!
  "Condemnation of Homosexual Acts": This explains the scholarly debate concerning, especially, *Romans 1:26-27.*

Rigney, Joe. *The Sin of Empathy: Compassion and its Counterfeits.* Moscow, Idaho: Canon

Press, 2025.
A traditionalist exposition of populist perceptions of progressive approaches.

Soughers, Tara K. *Beyond a Binary God: A Theology for Trans* Allies.* New York: Church Publishing, 2018.
Trans perspectives. My understanding is that the use of the asterisk is no longer preferred.

Stuckey, Allie Beth. *Toxic Empathy: How Progressives Exploit Christian Compassion.* New York: Penguin Random House LLC, 2024.
A traditionalist exposition of populist perceptions of progressive approaches.

White, E. B. *Stuart Little.* New York: HarperCollins Children's Books, 1945.
In addition to the Bible, every bibliography should include this masterpiece.

Web Articles and Podcasts

Akinwale, Funmi. *What is the REAL Meaning of 1 Timothy 2:12?*
https://whenyouneedgod.com/what-is-the-real-meaning-of-i-timothy-212-deep-dive-bible-study-commentary/ . Knoxville: 2022.
This commentary views 1 Timothy 2:12 as a directive for a specific community, possibly in response to false teachings and cultural dynamics, to limit disruptive behavior. The verse does not issue a universal ban against

female leadership. However, there should be a commandment against overloading a blog with so many ads.

Bass, Diana Butler. *Mary The Tower.* https://dianabutlerbass.substack.com/p/mary-the-tower . Harmony, North Carolina: 2022. Martha of Bethany, Mary Magdalene, and the Christological confession in John 11.

Distefano, Matthew J. *Saved From God? Alternatives to Penal Substitution Atonement Theory.* https://www.patheos.com/blogs/allsetfree /2018/01/saved-god-alternatives-penal-substitution-atonement-theory/. Sturgeon Bay, WI: 2021. This views *substitutionary atonement* as subordinate to *Christus Victor*. The former states that a wrathful God required the sacrifice of Jesus to provide atonement for our sins. The latter states that sin and death are defeated and do not prevent us from being one with God. See also Machen.

Galston, William A. *Trump, the Working Class, and Social Order.* The Wall Street Journal, New York, 5 August 2025. This opinion essay considers key foundations of social order, including organized religion.

Gold, Nicholas. *The Egalitarian Basis of Galatians 3:28: Unity Over Idolatrous Distinctions.*

https://www.cbeinternational.org/resource/
the-egalitarian-basis-of-galatians-328-
unity-over-idolatrous-distinctions/ . Christians
for Biblical Equality (CBE) International,
South Carolina: 2022.
Gold discourages idolatry, and I encourage
humility—interchangeable. Gold misses the
opportunity to mention the rebuttal of Socrates and the Talmud; see Palvanov.

Palvanov, Efraim. *On That Controversial Bless-
ing of "Not Making Me a Woman."*
https://www.mayimachronim.com/
on-that-controversial-blessing-of-not-
making-me-a-woman/ . 2019.
This article discusses the Talmudic morning
prayer in which a man thanks God for being
male, Jewish, and able to reason. The article
notes the similarity to the Greek saying attributed to Socrates expressing gratefulness
for being human, male, and Greek. Palvanov
does not give credit to the philosophical
weight of the rebuttal in Galatians, in which
Paul stated there is no Jew or Greek, no slave
or free, no male and female. Powell's text-
book makes this connection.

Sherman, Carter, WHYY radio, Tobias Hess,
Veralyn Williams.
https://www.npr.org/2025/06/23/1254614599/
carter-sherman-gen-z-sex. *Fresh Air*, audio,
Philadelphia: 2025.

This episode features a frank but controlled discussion of the American, Gen-Z approach to sex. This excludes the participation of a cisgendered straight man and thus favors a female and LGBTQ bias, but exposes objectivization, dehumanization, victimization, and reclusiveness caused by selfishness and insensitivity. The episode does not discuss spirituality.

Smith, Peter, Religion News Service.
https://religionnews.com/2025/03/17/
protestant-denominations-try-new-ideas-as-they-face-declines-in-members-and-money/.
Protestant denominations try new ideas as they face declines in members and money.
Washington, D.C.: 2025.
A 2025 article on the decline in attendance experienced by Christian denominations.

Research, in a manner of speaking.

Your intrepid author has visited Greece. I stood where Socrates thought great thoughts in the ancient Athenian Acropolis, and I climbed onto the rocky Areopagus next to the Parthenon where the council passed judgments. I followed the footsteps of Paul through ancient Corinth where visitors may stand on Gallio's bema.
https://gocekbloggary.gocek.net/2024/06/
in-footsteps-of-paul-in-corinth-greece.html

I am not a Talmudic scholar, but without further references, the Talmud states females do not require circumcision. Scholarly commentary on this suggests females already possess the holiness conferred to males through circumcision. However, my understanding is that circumcision establishes a male's connection to God and to the Jewish community in covenant with God, and this is a critically important ritual for a male. I just don't buy the notion that females are considered—by the Judaic canon—to be born with an equivalent connection to God, no circumcision needed. The ancient Hebrew scribes simply excluded females.

The New Testament establishes baptism in place of circumcision and does not comment on Judaism's lack of female circumcision. Judaism is not anti-female and females are well respected, but there is no canonical, Judaic equivalent to circumcision for females. Paul was one of the most eloquent philosophers in history, but even Paul couldn't avoid repeated references to circumcision to confirm his Jewish background and state that circumcision was not required for Christians. Subconscious or not, the patriarchal foundation of circumcision cannot be interpreted away. I give credit to the author of Colossians 2:11 for the non-sexist metaphor, *spiritual circumcision.*

THE ORCHESTRA: AN ALLEGORY

An orchestra conductor hired 200 musicians. At first, they all played in different musical keys, and even switched keys while playing. It sounded terrible. They held to an evil, selfish purpose, confident that in the large crowd no one could hear them individually.[1] The conductor convinced a dozen or so to play only in the key of C. In their corner of the orchestra, the sound was beautiful, but overall, the orchestra still sounded terrible.

After a while, musicians near the group playing in C heard the beautiful music, so they, too, switched to the key of C. Overall, the orchestra still sounded terrible, but it was better than before. Gradually, more and more musicians heard the beautiful sound and switched to the key of C, and the conductor was confident that on some future day, all people would behold how good and how pleasant it is for all to play together in unity[2].

After a long time, only a few stragglers still played in different keys. Previously, when only a few musicians played in the key of C, the conductor's options were limited; players were needed, so they pressed on through the cacophony. When almost all had switched to the key of C, the conductor rebuked the stragglers and they fled; the beauty of the sound of unity was as thunder to the stragglers, and they hurried away.[3]

[1] Ps 64:5, "They hold fast to their evil purpose; they talk of laying snares secretly, thinking, 'Who can see us?'"
[2] Ps 133:1, "How very good and pleasant it is when kindred live together in unity!"
[3] Ps 104:7, "At your rebuke they flee; at the sound of your thunder they take to flight."

ABOUT THE AUTHOR

Gary Gocek is a progressive lay Christian, worshiping in upstate New York (USA) with his wife, cats, and guitars. As of 2025, Gary has completed two years of *Education for Ministry*, a four-year, mentored program of theological reflection on the Bible, its historical context, and intersectional interpretations. EfM is sponsored by the Episcopal Church and its curriculum is maintained by the University of the South. Gary completed the two-week program of the *College for Congregational Development* in 2018. Gary earned a Bachelor of Science degree in Computer Science from the Rochester Institute of Technology and is a retired computing professional. Gary has surrendered to the wisdom of the Oxford comma.

https://gary.gocek.com/
When contacting Gary, include *Progressive* in email subjects and exclude profanity.

www.ingramcontent.com/pod-product-compliance
Lightning Source LLC
Chambersburg PA
CBHW070459050426
42449CB00012B/3038